D0122720

What is Architecture?
and 100 Other Questions

Rasmus Wærn & Gert Wingårdh

Published in 2015
by Laurence King Publishing Ltd
361–373 City Road
London EC1V 1LR
Tel +44 20 7841 6900
Fax +44 20 7841 6910
E enquiries@laurenceking.com
www.laurenceking.com

A catalogue record for this book is available
from the British Library

ISBN 978-1-78067-602-9

Originally published in Swedish as
Vad är arkitektur?
This edition published by arrangement with
Bokförlaget Langenskiöld
www.langenskiolds.se

Cover photo: Halmstad, Sweden

Design: Alexandre Coco

Printed in China

What is Architecture?

and 100 Other Questions

Rasmus Wærn & Gert Wingårdh

Photographs by Gerry Johansson
Translation by John Krause

Laurence King

Much of what is said in this book has been said before. Architects such as Adolf Loos expressed themselves with incomparable clarity on the distinction between art and architecture. Gunnar Asplund commented wisely on the style of a time and place, Bruno Taut on color and Jacques-François Blondel on architectural character. In this book, we have built further upon old wisdom, extending it to contemporary situations and coming up with some new ideas—the same process, in other words, that's used for making architecture.

Architects have been trying to describe the essence of architecture since antiquity, if not earlier. In contrast to other forms of art, architecture is often expected to explain itself. If it's going to be expensive, we deserve to know what we're paying for. In addition to the fundamental provision of utility and comfort, architecture can add commercial value for the client in many ways, including promoting an image, drawing publicity or generating revenue.

But its enigmatic essence goes beyond such benefits. What is that essence? We've come up with a hundred and one different ways to describe it.

Some of our answers may seem contradictory, which is just as it should be. The same question can have many different correct answers, as anyone who's been in a city will know. The subject is both so fun and so serious that it would be strange if either our buildings or our answers didn't span that entire spectrum. If this book can help the reader appreciate what a wonderful (and emotional) game architecture can be, we'll be very happy to hear about it—write us and let us know. And if you don't find an answer to your own question about architecture, you're welcome to email us and we'll try to answer it.

Photographer Gerry Johansson has also come up with answers to some of the questions. He has been documenting human buildings and their traces around the world for many years, and he chose some pictures from his archives that give even more depth to some of our answers. Seeing is the basis of all architectural work. Learning to see the things that elude a distracted observer has always been the foundation of the architect's training. The slow practice of drawing continues to be important in that regard. Gerry is just as slow in his work with large-scale film and big cameras. Few can sharpen their view by seeing the world through the lens like he can.

The text of this book is also the result of collaboration. We have talked, Rasmus has written, and Gert has pared it down. Discarding ideas is a core aspect of the modern practice of architecture. It is a culture that develops best through debate.

Rasmus Wærn and Gert Wingårdh
Stockholm and Gothenburg, Sweden

1

Why is the world most beautiful at twilight?

Short answer:

That's when the narrow logic of day gives way to the vast mystique of the night.

Long answer:

There is a kind of beauty in technical limitation: frost flowering on a poorly insulated window, algae blooming from damp concrete, and light sifting through the gaps in the wall of a barn. It's often moisture, the archenemy of the building arts, that causes problems in construction but, at the same time, approaching decay gives the built world a human dimension. A garden is never so beautiful as when touched by the wild. A house is never as lovely as when refined by the passage of time. Architecture can help us move on through life, to grow from the categorical certainties of childhood through the critical phase of adolescence and on to develop a sensitivity for the mystical in our lives. The beauty of dawn and dusk is hard to explain, but easy to destroy; you only have to switch on the light.

2

Thresholds: wouldn't it be nice to get rid of them?

Short answer:

It would. But then we would also lose a sense of transition.

Long answer:

It's not for nothing that the threshold has become such a powerful metaphor. It marks the boundary between inside and outside a room, but also the barrier that separates one state from another in any context. That difference is most tangible for those who depend on wheels for getting around. Society is striving to lower the thresholds that divide us and limit our options, and for the sake of the disabled it would be great to see thresholds eliminated entirely. But there's also a lot of important meaning in crossing over a threshold, especially a high one. If we choose to eliminate all the resistance represented by thresholds, we also lose some of the reward we feel when we cross from one side to the other.

3

How long will modernity be dressed in glass?

Short answer:

As long as you can claim that glass is almost nothing.

Long answer:

Ever since the Gothic era, glass has scored points for its invisibility. Walls of glass are often described using words such as openness, transparency, and participation. But those words are more compelling than the reality. In practice, a glass building can be just as forbidding as a blank wall. Glass buildings are as tangible as others and must be treated as such. We used to rely on window muntins to give form and substance to glass, weaving together the wall across the window opening. If glass is going to make up the whole wall on its own, it also has to be able to be *something*. That requires more than just wanting to be nothing.

4

When does architecture become sensual?

Short answer:

As soon as it moves you, especially in secret.

Long answer:

What is concealed is always enticing—and often delightful. When walls and openings create a rhythm of concealment and openness, architecture becomes irresistible. It has nothing to do with style. The allure of not being able to see everything all at once can be as powerful in a pavilion as in an apartment. A wall of glass that exposes the whole show to anyone who's interested is impressive, but it can't compare to the excitement of a glimpse through the gaps. The interplay between open and closed is the essence at the heart of architecture.

5

Can't we design buildings to look like they used to?

Short answer:

Sure we can. But everything will always bear the mark of its own time.

Potsdam, Germany

Long answer:

Sticking with something that we know works is a good strategy. Lots of old buildings and cities function extraordinarily well. As a rule it's dumb to replace them with something else. And modern times don't necessarily demand modern buildings. In many cases it's easy to live a modern lifestyle in a renovated building. The problem with creating new buildings and cities that look like old ones is not imitation per se—we've learned to deal with much bigger lies than that. But the charm of old cities runs deep below the surface. Once we've learned to really understand old buildings and cities, we can recreate their qualities in other forms. Buildings are resources; projects are opportunities.

6

Do buildings really have memories?

Short answer:

Buildings are the protein of memory.

Long answer:

Historical landmarks belong to a legacy
of collective memory. When we encounter
buildings where other lives once played
out, memories are freed up, released from
the walls where they have been resting for
years. Buildings can convey experiences
that go beyond an individual's memory. The
accumulation of experience is strengthened by
a characterful architecture and by preserving
buildings more or less intact. Damage to
a building is like damage to a database of
experience, which can create stress and
uncertainty. Even when they need to be torn
down, we must realize that buildings are much
larger than the physical volume they occupy.

7
What makes cities so fascinating?

Short answer:

They're really, really complicated.

Tokyo, Japan

Long answer:

Cities are the most complex things man has created. The most vital ones develop lives that differ from one neighborhood to another and from one city to another. That vitality depends on human behavior and how a city provides the conditions for life. The most important factor in the human animal's happiness is to feel recognized. If it feels like the buildings, the streets, the parks, and the plazas are there for our sake, we can usually accept that they might be congested, noisy, and time-consuming. Even ugly. Beautiful cities are nice, but it is hardly pastoral beauty that makes London and Tokyo two of the most charismatic cities in the world.

8

Doesn't technology determine everything?

Short answer:

No. That's a cover-up for what we lose when everything looks the same.

Long answer:

The Romans developed the stone arch to span over larger and larger openings, reaching far beyond what a single stone lintel would allow. A little more than a thousand years later, the French cathedral builders found that a pointed arch could be more graceful. The arch's form was its technology. Technology can be just as determining today—if we want it to. But because building construction has become so multi-faceted, we can always choose a different technique if the shoe doesn't fit. Architecture that gets its form from technology is usually called high-tech. But compared to nanotechnology or particle acceleration, it's pretty low-tech. Building is still a craft and its methods are there to be manipulated.

9

What caused the crisis in architecture?

Short answer:

It's hard for buildings to make something of themselves when no one believes they matter.

Long answer:

For a while, modern architecture was seen as a kind of necessary evil. It was a price we had to pay to achieve the other forms of excellence offered by modern living: weekends off, hospitals where one could get well, and parking places right underneath the office. As easy as it was to agree on those things, it was just as hard to agree on aesthetics. Since everyone seemed to have his or her own idea of what beauty was, the most rational approach was just to disregard the issue. Technocratic buildings had difficult beginnings; no one believed they were going to matter. But an unacceptably poor result quickly becomes an expensive one. It became necessary to form an opinion of what constitutes beautiful new architecture. But it's hard to decide what we want—especially before we've imagined it.

10

Is there some kind of universal formula?

Short answer:

Sometimes.
But not right now.

Long answer:

What's so unusual about contemporary architecture is that there is no definitive answer about what's right and what's wrong. On the one hand, this kind of freedom is very appealing—or at least it ought to be. But, on the other hand, it is hard to score when the goal posts are constantly moving. There is no room for error in one's ability to understand, design, explain, or build. Extraordinary architecture demands extraordinary skills. In the days when everyone knew what the rules were, as in the days of classicism, it was easier to get everyone marching together to the same beat. In architecture schools, students learned the rules for making beautiful buildings, which meant that anyone with a knack for studying could produce good architecture. And, because the solutions were all variations on known themes, it was rarely difficult to get them built according to the architect's intention. The fact that this kind of formula disappeared doesn't mean it can't come back. Do not underestimate the power of an idea that lasted for two thousand years.

11

Do architects have to think of everything?

Short answer:

Yes. That's exactly what architecture is.

Long answer:

While everyone else has their role to play, the architect needs to think about every line in the script. Only by understanding human behavior, as well as technology and art, is it possible to create buildings and spaces that really work. Many of the world's most famous buildings are full of shortcomings, but that hardly makes them failures. Fallingwater, Frank Lloyd Wright's world-famous house in Pennsylvania of 1935, leaked in fifty different places when it was new and later it almost collapsed under its own weight. Most of the building's problems were later fixed and the unparalleled artistry of the design made the substantial interventions worth the effort. Wright did the best he could. However, unlike technical problems, artistic shortcomings can seldom be corrected afterward.

12
How long
should
buildings
last?

Short answer:

The longer the better.

Ulan Bator, Mongolia

Long answer:

It doesn't take long before a building begins to change form, whether you want it to or not. First, a bunch of stuff gets put inside it. The interior ought to tolerate this to some extent, and many buildings do not come into their own until life begins to leave traces within them. For public buildings, the next change is when the furnishings start being replaced. Often, this is not an improvement. Rather than talking about how long buildings last, perhaps we should talk about their half-life. Like radioactive materials, architecture begins to degrade immediately. Public interiors have the shortest half-life. After just ten years, maybe only half of the original environment remains. Windows, doors, flooring, and everything else besides the structural frame, lasts a little longer, perhaps thirty years. And after sixty years there may only be half of the building left at all. But even when buildings are gone and replaced with others, the old urban plan is usually still there. It can last hundreds of years, sometimes even thousands.

13

Buildings frame our lives. But can life ever be predictable?

Short answer:

For a moment, until something happens.

Long answer:

Lives change and buildings with them.
Renovations and additions can harm a
building's artistic integrity, but change is an
inevitable part of life. Like people, buildings
can carry their experiences with dignity. There
are two ways to equip buildings for the changes
to come. One is to provide dimensions that
are so generous and floor plans that are so
general that they can be reorganized without
resorting to drastic interventions. For example,
the palaces of the seventeenth and eighteenth
centuries have proven suitable for most uses.
The other way is to use flexible construction
methods. For instance, walls might be moved
around beneath an extra high ceiling. Buildings
that live long are either very forgiving of life's
changes or so unique in their beauty that life
bends humbly to their will.

14
Someone took my idea. Should I be upset?

Short answer:

No, not if it was a good idea.

Reading, USA

Long answer:

There are artistic, ethical, and legal limits to how much architects (or any creative practitioners) can cut and paste. However, keeping track of what others are doing is just as important as being aware of the limits, because other people's ideas can make your own projects better. Architecture doesn't usually develop through invention, but rather through discovery. Reusing an old solution is one way of renewing architecture. Maintaining a general awareness of the world around you is also a way to identify the pitfalls you need to avoid. A more acute awareness allows us to make discoveries in all times and all places. But there is no reason to invent something if it's not an improvement.

15

Are natural materials better than imitations?

Short answer:

Yes. That's why they get imitated.

Long answer:

Materials that are taken directly from nature—wood, stone, clay, water, ice— have a different status than those that have undergone more or less complicated processes of transformation—concrete, steel, aluminum, glass, paper, plastic. Their character and their processes of aging exceed our powers of determination. If we use them just the way we found them, they at least have their integrity left. And in a world of speculation, integrity has an unbeatable elegance. Authentic materials can be expensive, but to some extent they are unavoidable. Not always everywhere, but always somewhere.

16
Does history have a future?

Short answer:

History is the only thing we know anything about.

Long answer:

History is always current, and there are three reasons for architects to have a good grasp of the past. First of all, almost all new buildings are built where others already exist. If we don't understand why they look the way they do, we are going to make some expensive mistakes. Second, there is poetry in the way a building relates to its own time. That poetry is easy to see but hard to create. And history is really the only guide we have through that elusive dimension. Third, architectural history is important because it can give us answers to the question of what architecture is. Mastering our history gives architects confidence and confidence is a good foundation to build on. In fact, it's the only one.

17
Can architecture be mass-produced?

Short answer:

It can. But the savings are at
the expense of diversity.

Emmaboda, Sweden

Long answer:

In the late 1920s Volvo introduced its first car and a prefab-house company its first house. At the time, they cost about the same. Today, a new prefab home costs about ten times as much as the cheapest Volvo automobile. The fact that we haven't been able to industrialize construction to the same extent as auto manufacturing has always irritated the construction industry, and they have often had the politicians on their side. A lot of things can be done both better and cheaper through mass production, but we have failed if the most lasting impression we have of our houses is how quickly they were constructed. If that old Volvo didn't make it into a museum, it's probably no longer around, while the house is probably still serving its purpose.

18
Is architecture necessary?

Short answer:

No. Some people will always be strong enough to make it anyway.

Long answer:

We can be uplifted by a beautiful and harmonious view of a city even though we know that, just like every other city, it is full of wretched, bickering, greedy, and dishonest people. But the shortcomings of its inhabitants do not spoil the joy of a divine urban scene. Likewise, you can grow up in an impoverished environment and still be an outstanding person. And even the most well-designed environment provides no guarantees about the quality of life. To believe otherwise is a form of determinism. As Winston Churchill said, "We shape our buildings; thereafter they shape us." Luckily, this is not always true. We push back, suppress the dreadful, mask over it, or we rebuild. If the architecture isn't there from the start it will come, as long as people get the chance to make their mark.

19

Does architecture develop?

Short answer:

No. On the other hand,
it never stands still.

Long answer:

Art does not develop. We cannot say that a later building is automatically better architecture than an earlier one. Technology, on the other hand, does develop, which is one reason why the conditions for architecture are continually changing. But those changes do not always mean artistic improvement. Architecture is built on experience. An architect needs to know lots of old tricks and know how to adapt them when the circumstances change. The job is about constantly trying to make everything a little better. But the field of architecture cannot rely on the fact that new buildings are more sophisticated than older ones. Without continuous artistic change, architecture becomes banal.

20
How can an architect become famous?

Short answer:

Fame is fleeting.
Aim for immortality.

Long answer:

Buildings—or at least their reputations—often outlive their creators. Even though all buildings are the result of work by a huge number of people, it is usually the architect's name that rises to the top. Unless the client puts their name on the façade (which is not unusual), it is the architect who embodies the work that goes into the project. That's because the architect's work is more personal than the client's, the city planner's, or the construction workers'. And we are attracted to the personal. If the architecture is good it gets attention. And the glow of its success shines on the architect. The creation glorifies its creator.

21

Why do people look at buildings when they're traveling?

Short answer:

Apparently we just cannot get enough of painstakingly sculpted buildings and cities.

Long answer:

There's nothing special about liking buildings, especially those that have been around long enough to ripen with beauty and to become a joy to the people around them. Driven by a longing to see how comfortably and pleasantly life can be lived, most of us enjoy strolling around among buildings that have been carefully designed and that, usually, have been preserved with great care as well. You cannot compare the popularity of art with that of architecture. Art asks questions; architecture answers questions. Art is uncomfortable; architecture is comfortable.

22

I read all the magazines and blogs. Is there anything I might have overlooked?

Short answer:

An experience, perhaps.

Long answer:

There's more to architecture than meets the eye. Sight is just one of our senses, but it has acquired a crushing dominance over the other impressions that enrich our lives. Think of all the beauty a hand can experience. You cannot see what you feel with your skin, but architecture that doesn't invite you to touch it remains forever sterile. And what would a cellar be without the cool, earth-scented air that waits in the darkness for us to open the door? Rich architecture can be felt, and smelled, and heard—it comes at you. A cathedral may look magnificent, but if it remained silent it would feel like a grave; its walls are there to lift aloft its music as well as its roof.

23
Does it have to be expensive?

Short answer:

Yes. Life is to be treasured.

Long answer:

It is always alarmingly expensive to build, whether for individuals or for countries. Cost is an eternal challenge for architecture, even though the discipline is essentially about achieving the greatest benefit for the least possible cost. A quality result demands a disciplined austerity. But there's a difference between austerity and value engineering. Value engineering is about taking advantage of opportunities, or about being forced to adapt. That is an art in itself, but it only gets noticed during the planning. After the building is finished, both the costs and the cost savings are forgotten. Austerity, in contrast, refines a project and lends it beauty throughout the life of the building. You should never skimp on the austerity. Parsimony, on the other hand, breeds lasting discontent.

24
Can you own a view?

Short answer:

No, you can only borrow it.

Fjärås, Sweden

Long answer:

The Japanese garden is typically conceived as a universe unto itself. Only in exceptional cases do they "borrow the landscape" in the way that has become the norm in the West. A Western garden is oriented outward. It's nice to have a beautiful view, especially of things we associate with leisure—such as waterfronts, mountains, and plazas with café seating—but there's a particular delight in having an experience tantalizingly hidden. When Le Corbusier and Salvador Dalí designed a roof terrace in Paris for the eccentric multi-millionaire Carlos de Beistegui, they screened off the spectacular view so that only half of the Arc de Triomphe was visible. If you have enough self-confidence, you don't bother with borrowing landscapes.

25
Is it important to get published?

Short answer:

It's a big deal for the architect,
but even bigger for the building.

Long answer:

Getting published is just about the only way for either the architect or the building to make a name for themselves. Publicity brings the architect new clients. It also increases the value of the building and, therefore, its life span. That's nothing new. The need to show and to read about buildings has existed as long as it has been possible to circulate pictures and text. Renaissance illustrations cross-fertilized the orient with the occident, the books of the Enlightenment spread images of the Far East throughout Europe and, with the advent of photography, illustrations became the focus of the creative process of building. Only tradition is refined without publicity. Architecture is built on memories and images.

26
Do books give you a sharper view?

Short answer:

Books point things out and explain them. But you still have to do the looking yourself.

Long answer:

When the author August Strindberg visited Rome in 1885, he knew what to expect before he arrived. His tour was merely a repetition of what he'd read in books. He had already learned all about the monuments. "Rome wasn't built in a day, but it can be disposed of in one," was his laconic comment to the driver of his non-stop tour of the city. By contrast, when the emperor Constantine came to Rome and saw Trajan's Forum, he stood in wonder over its unrivaled edifices as though struck by lightning. Unlike Strindberg, Constantine hadn't exhausted his curiosity for Rome with reading. Seeing made him swoon; Strindberg was only there to *have* seen.

27

What protects us from becoming blind to everyday wonders?

Short answer:

The imagination.

Long answer:

Beauty is everywhere, but in everyday life we
only see the familiar details. So uninteresting!
If you admire a view with your guests, you'll
know the name of everything you see: buildings,
neighborhoods, mountains, lakes. Your guests,
knowing nothing of these places, will instead
be struck by the rhythm of the landscape, the
color of the sky, and perhaps the odd detail.
The virgin experience is a luxury—it tempts us
to travel in search of more. Only when you meet
the world with your eyes wide open can you be
struck by the general aspects that characterize
any phenomena, from the European city to
the desert to the Nordic landscape. Few
buildings present vistas that always offer new
perspectives, but this is still the core of the art
of building—to get us continually to experience
the world anew.

28

What do buildings sound like?

Short answer:

Good buildings sound quiet.

Long answer:

A concrete frame transmits the pounding of
a pneumatic drill all the way into your bones.
A wooden box can project the vibration from
strings into the air around it. Played in a concert
hall, the tone can be flavored by the room's
timber lining. A stone vault is the strongest voice
in the choir and the empty echo of a vacated
room fills anyone with melancholy. When a
home is undressed, it loses its private sounds.
Quality also has a more objective tone: just as
the sound a car door makes when you close it
indicates the quality of the chassis, solid rooms
respond to our presence with a reassuringly
substantial voice, but only when spoken to.
Well-conceived buildings don't jabber.

29
Are all churches architecture?

Short answer:

No—but a sanctuary's
ambition gives it
a head start.

Västergötland, Sweden

Long answer:

When the first churches appeared, it was the
beginning of an art of building that continues
to invite new interpretations to this day. No
building type has been more influential.
Although a church's function is quite simple—
the sanctuary is essentially a lecture hall—its
architecture is expected to convey something
heavenly. The fact that places of worship were
built with greater care and were preserved more
intact than most other buildings puts them in
a class of their own. And, in modern times, it
is a remarkable fact that churches have been
more important to architecture in secular
Scandinavia than anywhere else in the world.
All of these structures are vessels for ideas
about light, sound, space, and movement. Some
perform this art with unearthly success.

30

Why do architects want to paint the world white?

Short answer:

It's easy.

Long answer:

Snow-white walls can elevate a space. But painting everything white is also a lazy strategy. Using color requires more dedication. But the connection between white paint and modernism is, in part, founded on a misunderstanding. Many early-modern buildings appeared much simpler in the black-and-white pictures published in international design magazines than they were in person. Modernism came to life in the hands of a group of architects who were colorful in every sense of the word. Every color influences a space and the people in it. Dark rooms should have darker colors and brightly lit ones should have brighter colors. Working with nature rather than against it is a good principle but, as Groucho Marx said, "Those are my principles, and if you don't like them … well, I have others."

31
Can a rich architecture be affordable?

Short answer:

Of course.
Rich architecture is complex.
Poor architecture is complicated.

Long answer:

Wealth does not necessarily create rich architecture. The natural response to the complexity of contemporary societies is to simplify. The need for a comprehensible environment fosters a desire for solutions that are simple—if not in depth, at least on the surface. However, a complex architecture, full of sensible contradictions, does seem to reflect a rich soul rather than a thick wallet.

32

What is the worst thing about architecture today?

Short answer:

Ceilings.

Long answer:

Ceilings have devolved from being the focal point of a room to being a zone for mechanical equipment. In all the world's greatest spaces we've always looked up in awe. Where our gaze was once met with fantastical vaulted ceilings, remarkable truss structures, or distinctive decorative treatments, today we typically find acoustic tiles, ductwork, and fluorescent strip lighting. Having abandoned the ceiling as a canvas for creativity with the dawn of the technological era, we've had a hard time taking it back. Today, it's hard to compete with all that mechanical equipment when all you're arguing for is a blank white surface. But a compelling vision of a space designed to make the ceiling its primary feature can enchant even the most pragmatic minds. There is good reason to be stubborn: since we seldom rearrange or redecorate the ceiling the way we do the rest of a space, what we create overhead lives a long life.

33

What is the best thing about architecture today?

Short answer:

That it's okay to be discreet.

Long answer:

Architecture has always had an ambiguous relationship with nature. On the one hand, it's adversarial: the building must keep the destructive forces of nature at bay. On the other hand, it's a love affair: what nature has to offer is simply limitless. In a few rare cases, architecture has been strong enough to meet nature with no mitigating, intervening boundary: the Greek temple, sprung from the rock on which it stands, is enclosed by nothing more than its stone columns, and the traditional Japanese house hovers above the landscape with its broad verandas and rice-paper walls. These archetypal forms set aside the common comforts of a controlled, indoor climate, but with today's technology it is possible to have an intimate relationship with nature without sacrificing comfort and shelter from the elements. The ability to make intelligent, responsive buildings that endure precisely because they can adapt is the greatest advancement of our era of building construction.

34

How is a beautiful façade composed?

Short answer:

Use only one window.

Long answer:

A façade that is loaded with forms and colors is necessarily cluttered. The effect can be charming in its own way. A frontage that is limited to a single material and nothing else will inevitably be austere. And it will often be handsome, especially if the material is beautiful. The real world is designed between these two extremes. Both the disorderly and the minimalist can be dreary, but you have a better chance of creating something beautiful if you're aiming for austerity than for excess. However, reduction must be refined with beautiful proportions. A sense for proportion takes hard work and demands severe self-criticism.

35

What is the point of regulations?

Short answer:

They prevent the worst.

Long answer:

On the other hand, they may also prevent the best—for example, a beautiful house on a coast where no one was allowed to build. But even if one or two well-designed houses along the shoreline are nice, a thousand would surely be disastrous. It is impossible to formulate a just law that says a few of us are entitled to build something that others are not, so instead we say no to everyone. Our regulations prevent construction in protected natural areas and they prevent radical urban transformations, but they also prevent almost everything that went into creating traditional cities. All of a project's qualities can be regulated except the sensual ones. Everyone loves to hate regulations. We can't get rid of them, but we can dream of getting an exemption. Art lives in the exception.

36

Is architecture the spice of life or its sustenance?

Short answer:

The soul can die of starvation too.

Long answer:

There is architecture and there is Architecture. The lowercase architecture works with types and deals with refining a type, particularly in residential design, rather than inventing a new one. Taken together, these buildings form a more or less nutritious foundation for our daily lives. We find Architecture, we hope, in society's most public buildings. They are carefully crafted dishes that strive for new sensations. We need to distinguish between architecture and Architecture. The former creates our environment; the latter, our milieu, the very center of our life. Both are crucial.

37

Is higher density always a good thing?

Short answer:

Of course not.
Yet, cities are fantastic.

Huskvarna, Sweden

Long answer:

Man's ability to adapt to different environments
is unmatched. But of all the different
environments we've made our own, the city
seems to suit us best. Being closely surrounded
by other people can try our nerves and lead
to conflict, but the advantages generally
outweigh the chafing. That's why we continue
to gather so tightly together and to press our
buildings together, too. But a lively urban street
atmosphere is something else entirely. That
depends on the number of people outside—not
inside—the buildings.

38

Art always wants to do the opposite. Is it the same with architecture?

Short answer:

No. Architecture isn't about either/or, it's about both/and.

Long answer:

The fact that rarities are viewed as exclusive is simply a product of man's inherent vanity. Where working outdoors is the norm, pale skin becomes the ideal, and vice versa. If harbors and seas are workplaces, cities turn their backs on their waterfronts. When we start using water for leisure and luxury, those same cities quickly turn themselves inside out. With industrialization, nature ceased to be a part of our everyday lives and the romantic landscape park became a new ideal. We could identify other reasons why things that used to be important later become marginalized. None of them, however, is as powerful as our need to compensate for the inescapable limitations life places on us.

39

Should architects build on the best place on the site?

Short answer:

No, next to it.

Brålanda, Sweden

Long answer:

Just because architecture is based on place doesn't mean the landscape is the only storyteller. Architecture must capture more dimensions than just its footprint. On a map, the big elements stand out: for example, the terrain beyond the trees. That's a reason not to see the site before you start designing. Distance stimulates analysis. The site is never constant; it bends to meet its new challenge. The sun, the wind, and the ground endure. Even before you've taken in a site and all its meaning, they can offer some immutable insights.

40

Who was the first architect?

Short answer:

Not Imhotep, anyway.

Long answer:

Imhotep was a universal man, a multi-talented genius of the twenty-seventh century BCE in Egypt. He designed the first pyramid and was eventually elevated to a god. His position in the history of architecture is hard to beat, but of course there were architects before him. Imagine the moment when the first animal hides were laid out on the ground. A place that a moment before had been unfocused and undifferentiated, but full of possibilities, suddenly took on a definite shape. The hides established a center, a place in front of them, and a place behind them. And when stones were then arranged on the ground around them, the first designed space was born.

41

How are the conditions for architecture where I live?

Short answer:

Good! Optimism is essential to life.

Long answer:

The quality of the architecture in a country or
a region is carried on four pillars. The first is
a collective self-confidence: without a sense of
pride among architects, clients, and builders,
it's hard for architecture to take off. The
second pillar is a decent economy. Too much
money in too little time does more harm than
good, but a stable situation provides the basis
for building for the future. The third pillar
of good architecture is the number of special
commissions—those in which the design is
driven by qualities other than the price.
The fourth pillar is individual talent: without
Antoni Gaudí, Barcelona would not have
become such a marvel a hundred years ago.
The times and places that have given rise to
legendary architecture have had all four pillars
at once, but it's still possible to make history if
one of them happens to topple.

42

Is it strange that we long to get away sometimes?

Short answer:

No. All building begins with longing.

Long answer:

The feeling of longing is stronger than that of having. Since antiquity, longing for other places and other times has given us the most inspiring environments created by man. Built images of Italy, Turkey, or China are sometimes more fascinating than the real thing. The most enduring of all dreams is the dream of Greece. The Romans dreamed of Greece, Le Corbusier dreamed of Greece, and for the nineteenth-century Scottish architect Alexander "Greek" Thomson, Greece was a vision he never actually experienced. Western cultures rest on Arcadian dreams.

43

Must we demolish beautiful buildings and scenic vistas in order to urbanize?

Short answer:

No, why should we?
Architecture is urbanization
with a human face.

Long answer:

Urbanization has improved living conditions
for many people, but it has also wiped out
many beautiful traces of human endeavor.
A rising standard of living always calls attention
to the inadequacy of the built environment.
Higher standards and greater demand create
conflicts—they take a toll on people and on
capital. Architects who work with developers are
guilty by association in the eyes of the public,
but as practicing professionals they are often
the first to appreciate the qualities of the built
environment when it becomes threatened, and
hopefully also to see the opportunities to create
something even better. The conflict between
preservation and renewal has raged through
every architect and through every city that's
demolished its way forth. This will inevitably
continue, but it's always reasonable to demand
that the new give more than it takes.

44

A swimming pool lined with fake fur? Sounds terrible, doesn't it?

Short answer:

Not necessarily.

Long answer:

Imagine seaweed. It is beautiful and yet just
a bit disconcerting, because you can never be
completely certain what is hiding in it. That
is one of those qualities of nature that are
hard to transfer to architecture. But it is easy
to be inspired by the suppleness and fluidity
of seaweed and, for anyone who dares to look
beyond the conventional, there is a lot of
beauty to discover hidden in the so-called ugly.
The built environment seldom fits neatly into
categories of good or bad. The steel skeleton
of a half-finished building, the jagged pit of
a stone quarry, and the coarse simplicity of
a brick wall all make a straightforward and
unapologetic impression. A self-confident beast
of a building may turn out to be more reliable
than a coquettish beauty.

45

What is the cleverest way to save money?

Short answer:

Make it small.

Long answer:

Buildings are expensive. Big buildings are very expensive, smaller buildings less so. In the end, even the thriftiest among us can never save as much by cutting corners as is wasted by building too big. The most expensive things to build, like spaces below the water table, are usually hidden from view; and the most visible, like the finished surfaces, have only a marginal impact on the total cost. The efficient use of space is therefore the most cost-effective and eco-friendly feature we can give a building. And that's exactly why big spaces are among the most wonderful, grandiose and generous features a building can offer us.

46

Why is there so much prestige attached to an opera house?

Short answer:

Because the expectation of its performance inevitably includes its architecture.

Long answer:

The Berlin Opera, completed in the middle of the eighteenth century, was the first free-standing theater house in Europe to play a principal role in the heart of the city; the court theaters that preceded it were, as a rule, adjacent to palaces or city blocks, and free theaters, such as Shakespeare's Globe, tended to be located in the outskirts. Its free placement was also an indication of the theater's increasing independence in relation to the Prussian Court, and it was no coincidence that the audience could be referred to for the first time as "the public," since they were members of the general population. All of this is indicative of what an important role theater buildings played in cities throughout the Western world. The opera house, as a type, housed such a complex art form that it rapidly became the most distinctive cultural landmark in many other capitals. It represents public life in its most refined form.

47
What is stone?

Short answer:

Stone is forever.

Long answer:

Stone is more of a symbol than a construction
material. That's why the central urban
buildings of Europe used to imitate real
stone architecture. The legacy we have of
the great building traditions is made up of
stone buildings. Even from cultures where the
primary construction material was actually
wood, the monuments are of stone. When
nineteenth-century builders in Europe wanted
to add credibility to their hastily constructed
housing developments, they imitated stone.
It's a paradoxical material: on the one hand,
it is heavy and solid; on the other, it is used
almost exclusively, nowadays, as a thin cladding.
Nothing could be more basic than rock, or more
luxurious. Natural stone is durable in some
ways, fragile in others. It communicates a sense
of patient craftsmanship. The material awakens
in us today the same kinds of associations it did
in the nineteenth century.

48

Why are ruins so beautiful?

Short answer:

They are romantic.

Long answer:

The essence of romance lies in provoking strong feelings. This sense goes beyond the reach of dime-store novels. Buildings can also invoke a momentous, solemn gravity, especially ruins in moonlight. Ruins reveal what's left of a building: its primary geometry. Every wall bears witness to an accumulation of work. Its collapse makes the impermanence of our greatest efforts so much clearer, because anyone can see that the ruin will never be reconstructed. If a well-preserved building reveals our vain dreams of immortality, the ruin is a manifestation of the reality of life. Everything we love will one day be gone— people, buildings, cities, and trees. You mourn and move on.

49

What is architecture?

Short answer:

The built image of ourselves.

Long answer:

In a world of fluid, virtual values, architecture endures. The images that you, your work, your city, and your country create by building will more than likely outlive you. Buildings are the most important traces we leave behind as people. Old ones were here long before we arrived and the new ones we make will be here long after we're gone. Architecture is a collective selfie. It's a status that can't be updated.

50
What does urban mean?

Short answer:

There's no short answer to that question. Complexity is always throwing a wrench into simplicity's works.

Long answer:

Density may be a city's distinguishing feature.
It's a manifestation of our collective nature
as human beings. But it's not the whole truth
about life in the city. The vitality of a city is a
function of countless factors and, among them,
proximity is more important than density. If we
plan new neighborhoods based solely on the
idea of density, we run the risk of getting the
worst of both worlds—the cramped dimensions
of downtown *and* the desolation of the suburbs.
The style of its buildings has no impact on how
a city works. But other features do, such as street
connectivity, pedestrian entrances, ground-floor
commercial spaces, and expressive features.
Why it's so hard to achieve these things is
another question.

51

Why is it so hard to make good cities?

Short answer:

All the forces for good
are aligned against it.

Long answer:

The sum of all our benevolent regulations can often lead to the antithesis of a good city. It's a problem that many people, with marginal success, have tried to correct. All of our well-meaning standards with regard to noise reduction, safety, air quality, daylight, and parking add up to something that is far removed from a decent city. The fact that the product of modern real-estate economics equates to a dismal city is even harder to come to terms with. Although everyone is in agreement, for example, that institutions of higher education in downtown locations are beneficial in creating a great city, these institutions are often driven out when those areas become so attractive that the rent becomes unaffordable. If the city is to prosper as a whole, it can't be prosperous in every one of its parts.

52

What is the point of architectural competitions?

Short answer:

To distinguish
concept from creator.

Long answer:

The architecture of competitions has a
character all its own. The creativity that is
unleashed in a competition gives a client
the courage to pursue the kind of bold
architecture they probably wouldn't have
commissioned otherwise. Modern architecture
is therefore inseparably linked to architectural
competitions, just as modern society is linked
to competition itself. The fact that most of the
work that goes into these competitions comes to
nothing is inherent in the democratic process:
it is only by making many alternatives that we
know what we should reject. Political parties,
advocacy organizations, and architecture firms
are always developing strategic alternatives they
never get paid for and never use. On the other
hand, totalitarian states can be recognized
by their rigid architecture: it's impressive but
predictable, the opposite of the publicly vetted
solutions generated by competitions.

53

Is it okay to repeat yourself?

Short answer:

A good song is good
enough to be sung again.

Long answer:

Good solutions should be repeated. To repeat the words of Alvar Aalto, you can't invent a new style every Monday. At the same time, new one-off solutions attract more attention than recycled ones. The tension between the typical and the unique is the essence of urban development. Residential buildings are all variations on familiar themes—and they should be. They don't need to be interesting; they need to be good. Public buildings, on the other hand, must be distinctive. How distinctive? Just enough to be heard above the choir. Whether architects repeat themselves or reveal new sides of themselves every time is not that important. Not that many people are going to see more than one of their buildings anyway.

54

The opportunities seem infinite. If an architect could highlight just one quality, what should it be?

Short answer:

Light.

Long answer:

All architecture that makes a lasting impression works with daylight; how it falls on a surface, the play of shadows, the way it brings out a line, a material or a relief is central to the art of architecture. It's an awareness that can be found in every culture and every era. Daylight is free, but it has taken tremendous efforts to create the temples, auditoriums, homes, and palaces in which the design is driven by the conscious manipulation of light. And then there are the spaces where the wonder of light seems to emerge all on its own—through the spotted shadows of foliage, the gloom of a cave, or the faint glow of an igloo.

55

Where does form come from?

Short answer:

The law of gravity.

Long answer:

Everything wants to fall down. How buildings can remain upright is a technical problem. How they can appear to want to remain where they belong is an aesthetic problem. Gravity has always been a foundation of architecture, but more in the Western world than in Japan or Polynesia, where building construction is based on frames rather than walls. Today, buildings all over the world are shell structures built up of layer after layer, each with its own function. Gravity doesn't automatically give them character; temperament has to be designed in. Gravity must be confirmed, or challenged— heavy or light, bearing or borne. Life or death.

56
What role does politics play?

Short answer:

It establishes priorities.

Long answer:

In a description of how to deal with the human condition, Niccolò Machiavelli offered three key words that are still relevant today: the necessary, the possible, and the unpredictable. Once upon a time, the necessary conditions for cities were established by experts empowered by the state. Today, the power of municipal authorities is more about dealing with the possible in order to achieve as much as they can of the necessary. Nevertheless, the city is formed mostly by the unpredictable, in whose hands many large projects rest.

57

Has architecture become international?

Short answer:

Architecture has always been international.

Long answer:

All over the world, people look abroad when commissioning architecture in hopes of achieving a building that seems to be unique. Globalization is usually portrayed as progressive, while the regional is associated with the anti-modern and marginal. But great architecture is often rooted in local tradition, as with the Florentine Renaissance or the more modern Chicago and Glasgow schools. Ideas spread far and wide: magazines, books, travel, exhibitions, and competitions have conveyed ideas and forms from one place to another as long as they've existed. Borders mean nothing; what matters are climate, terrain, and society. When globalization is criticized, it's usually for its uncontrolled influence rather than for the privilege of making choices without regard to borders. And yet the two are inextricably linked.

58

Does a place have a soul?

Short answer:

No, it has several.

Norrsundet, Sweden

Long answer:

Places are characterized by nature and by nurture. They bear their geological inheritance in silence, but are acculturated by weather and by people. A dramatic birth and an extreme childhood create places of strong character. In such places, building is a delicate matter. Where architecture ought to refrain from asserting its power with raw force, it can still gather up the energy of the landscape with even the subtlest gesture. If the character of the site is more elusive, the responsibility to interpret it is all the greater. The first building on a site always creates a contrast. It can wipe out the relationships that make the place special. But, with the right touch, the history of the terrain, its weather, and the traces left by man can all be made visible. The character of its soul has changed and the building itself becomes a part of its history.

59

What is the world's most admired building?

Short answer:

The Crystal Palace.

Long answer:

The Crystal Palace was a magnificent cast-iron and glass structure built in London for the Great Exhibition of 1851. It stood in Hyde Park for a summer and, when the exhibition was finished, it was moved to Sydenham Hill, south London, where it was eventually consumed by fire in 1936. The building had a mythic influence. It was the dream of modernity made real for a moment. Pictures of the building hung on the walls of farmhouses far off in Germany. It was a building of more than eighty thousand square meters in area, so vast that the park's fully grown trees could be accommodated inside it. It completely changed the conception of what a building was. Greenhouses had been built with the same form before, but instead of housing plants this was meant for growing man's preeminence in the world. Such a profound change in the idea of what a building is had never been achieved before—or since. Rest in peace, Crystal Palace.

60

How small can a home be?

Short answer:

Like a sailboat.

Moskosel, Sweden

Long answer:

A small sailboat can make a good home because
it's so well designed, but also because the sea is
so vast. The endlessness of the horizon requires
ballast for balance. Living in a thoroughly
tight and enclosed world, on the other hand,
is punishing. Any room is, by nature, a limit to
freedom, but there are ways of compensating
for that. Surrounded by the open expanse
of the sea, life inside a boat demands great
care in the details, in the carpentry, and in
the materials in order to compensate for the
lack of space. But comfort is not merely the
absence of discomforts—that would be a hollow,
technocratic kind of comfort.

61

How do architects win competitions?

Short answer:

By understanding the client better than anyone else.

Long answer:

The client doesn't know what kind of architecture they want. If they did, they wouldn't need the architect. To win a competition, an architect has to come up with the best plan, and to do that they need to have more knowledge than anyone about what the client really wants, deep down. The architect also needs an expert jury that can understand and communicate the scheme's qualities; a winning proposal needs a good advocate. Most of the participants are essentially extraneous and most of the submissions are excluded with the first review. It hurts to get left out, but to compete in architectural competitions you just have to get used to it.

62
What is a good plan?

Short answer:

One that gives you the most possible benefit with the least possible means.

Long answer:

A good plan is effective. The rooms interlock
with one another so smoothly that unnecessary
steps are completely eliminated. The plan
choreographs our movements through space
and, inside buildings, these movements occur
almost exclusively on foot. The elevator and
the wheelchair are the biggest changes to the
floor-planning system since the stairway and
the door. Central heating liberated interiors
from the chimney and electricity transformed
the window from a light source into a view, but
it was only when the way we move changed that
buildings and cities began to take on completely
new forms. The elevator, the bus, and the car
have fundamentally shaken up the old truths
about what makes a good plan. The new ways of
moving are still searching for the right form.

63

Is there something special about marble?

Short answer:

Yes. Nothing is as devastating for artistic liberty as a good reputation.

Skånes-Fagerhult, Sweden

Long answer:

No other construction material can come close to the status of marble. The concept of marble, even more than the stone itself, exudes luxury and nobility. Until the industrial era, marble was the most practical stone type for large-scale application; although it's tough to saw and polish marble by hand, it is possible. Granite was impossibly difficult to work with until the advent of diamond-tipped machines made it a viable competitor, but by then marble had already had a couple of thousand years to secure its position as the diva of all construction materials. Its suitability as flooring for school cafeterias never spoiled that prestige. The most important attribute a material can have is its ability to awaken feelings in us.

64

Why is uncompromising architecture so good?

Short answer:

Because it's beautiful when everything works together.

Long answer:

Many of the most admired places in architecture
are monumentally uncompromising, including
the Place des Vosges in Paris, St. Peter's
Square in Rome, and Amalienborg Palace in
Copenhagen. They rise above the everyday and
emphatically proclaim man's authority to shape
the world. Their monumentality is due more to
their uncompromising confidence than to their
size. Repetition, monochromy, continuity, and
typologies have the ability to create harmony
at every scale.

65

Why is uncompromising architecture so bad?

Short answer:

Because people aren't all alike.

Long answer:

When we search for signs of human life among the long, blank boxes built in the 1960s, we often have to be content with signs, advertisements, and storefronts. In that era of record-breaking housing production, the sense of proportion was sold out for an uncompromising aesthetic of repetition. Uniformity can be incomparably handsome, but it has a kind of built-in insensitivity. Columns on the march will not yield. The temples of the Gothic era are no less rational than the repetitive, mathematical architecture of antiquity, but their wealth of variation elevated the individual above the mass of humanity. Repetition is great, as long as it is kept within limits.

66

What is the point of details?

Short answer:

Their presence.

Stockholm, Sweden

Long answer:

The experience of architecture is not
diminished when the dimensions are smaller.
On the contrary, it's in the details that we
can feel a building with our skin, and it's
therefore in the details that our bodies are most
intimately connected to it. Civilization today is
a culture of images, but architecture's means
of expression go well beyond the visual. A door
handle is felt not just in the surface of the form,
but also in the spring of the latch, the weight
of the door, and the precision of the hardware.
Whether the details are mass-produced
or not is of little consequence, as building
construction today has a hard time measuring
up to the manufacturing industry when it
comes to precision and delivery. But, to avoid
turning from designers into process managers,
architects must master the design of details.

67

What is the significance of tuberculosis?

Short answer:

Two billion infected and the advent of sanitary architecture.

Long answer:

Disease and war, more than anything else, have driven our desire to protect ourselves. The difficulty of containing tuberculosis led to many profound changes. Raising buildings on high bases was a way to avoid fetid air. Slick, hygienic surfaces, often of steel, would never have made their aesthetic breakthrough if not for the fight against tuberculosis. Old buildings were leveled to let in sun and fresh air, and new ones built—not just those trend-setting sanatoriums, but entire neighborhoods—to let in sun and fresh air. Nothing, except maybe war, has had a greater impact on architecture than tuberculosis.

68

I like interiors that are bright and cheery. Who doesn't?

Short answer:

It depends on when you happen to be reading this book.

Long answer:

When Sigmund Freud moved from Vienna to London, he brought his office with him, intact, down to the last detail. He saw no reason to change something that was working, and no reason to create intentionally any more change in his life than living in exile would force upon him. Freud's office, with its famous sofa, was dull and gloomy. Just as its shadows protected the room from exposing everything at once, the room itself took care of the souls who reclined on that sofa and were expected to open doors into the dark spaces hidden within themselves. It was as functional as you could get in the midst of the sundrenched functionalist era. Maybe sun and fresh air could chase away tuberculosis, but Freud trusted in dusk for getting into man's deepest recesses. A light is more brilliant in the dark.

69

What is noise?

Short answer:

An evaluation.

Long answer:

A city is seldom quiet. Some might see this as a problem, but it's hard to achieve the kind of city whose streets are lined with residential buildings. The demand for protecting rooms, at least bedrooms, from noise has grown in step with the increase in traffic. The most rational approach would be to keep housing and traffic separated by green space, but that makes streets feel like isolated traffic arteries. It reduces one conflict but creates others, including the loss of intimate street space. A city is fundamentally an enormous system for managing conflict. There have always been rules. Cities were much noisier in the Middle Ages than today, but only during the day. At night they were quiet. Completely quiet.

70

What makes old factories so cool?

Short answer:

They don't try too hard.
They just are.

Kvänum, Sweden

Long answer:

Post-industrial society handed over its factories to culture. Its vacant halls attracted music, theater, and exhibitions. Art could romp around in an oversized and tattered suit meant for hard physical labor. But it wasn't just the straightforward design that gave these spaces their intense character. Industry's need for expansive spaces and plenty of daylight, and its excess of heat, led to the creation of well-proportioned spaces built with robust materials, yet lit by slender and elegant windows. The early industrial plants, such as breweries, often imitated castles and fortresses, but soon the influence was reversed and housing began to mimic the ribbon windows, flat roofs, and smooth walls of factories. The straightforward attitude, however, could not be budged.

71
Is architecture natural?

Short answer:

No. Nature can only create shelter.

Long answer:

For at least the last five hundred years, nature has been foremost among the principles to which architects refer. Nature has been seen as the source of beauty, as the root of all architecture, as an ideal to be imitated, as freedom from cultural obligations, and now as an ecosystem on which architecture must have as little impact as possible. With the advent of modernism, nature began to be perceived as architecture's opposite. The pioneers of modernism saw it as their job to dominate the forces of nature, including gravity. The reason was not just that it had become technically feasible: without buildings neither civilization nor even the human species can survive. That's a pretty reasonable point of departure for design.

72
Do buildings have character?

Short answer:

Some have it from the beginning, others acquire it with time, and still others just can't keep their lack of character to themselves.

Long answer:

It's common to speak of a building's character. This book does it all the time. Character has been part of the game for ages—perhaps most notably since the eighteenth century, with the publication of a comprehensive catalogue of architecture's thirty-eight types of character, including sublime, noble, free, manly, light, delicate, naïve, feminine, mystical, ambivalent, and barbaric. It was a kind of manual, you might say. We need a lot of words for describing architecture. Even an architecture that is built on scientific principles, reliant on facts, and which is meant to rise above all subjective evaluation, quickly reveals its distinct character.

73

Are words necessary? Isn't it enough just to design?

Short answer:

Everything starts with words.

Long answer:

Architects spend more time talking, writing, listening, and reading than they do drawing. Buildings and towns are created through mutual understanding (and to some extent misunderstanding). The process for coming to an agreement is verbal. For a building to come out as its architects intend, they need more than just a compelling vision—they need strong arguments as well. A picture alone has never won a debate. Planning is a tremendous group effort, with drawing as a kind of script to record it. And yet, strangely enough, the language of the architect is often no more precise than that of the wine critic.

74
Does architecture have a moral?

Short answer:

Form is never a coincidence.
It's completely serious, always.

Long answer:

For modernist architects, nothing was more important than ensuring the *truth* of their work. They were supposed to be true to their artistic convictions, honest about the technology underlying the work, and frankly consistent with their own time. Since there was no room for more than one truth at a time, these demands eventually became unworkable. How could a multi-dimensional architecture avoid being false in at least some aspect? The moralists of the twentieth century were able to demolish, or at least scrape off, most of the showy glitz put up in the nineteenth. The "truth" they left was no more beautiful, only more dull. Our tolerance for extravagance has grown since then, but that doesn't mean morality has disappeared, only that our values have changed. Every era has its own morals; sustainability is the primary one in ours. Only deception is eternally unethical. An architect has to believe in what they do.

75

What is simplicity?

Short answer:

The antidote to excess.

Brålanda, Sweden

Long answer:

By the 1990s, the hunt for originality was being called "the usual unusual." The journal that coined the phrase wanted to see more of "the unusual usual," that is, an architecture that charges ordinary buildings with an extraordinary energy. That is difficult. Simplicity requires a wealth of variety if it is to avoid being banal. Providing an optimized frame for the simple life has been a primary challenge for architects of every era. This search is related to the simplicity of standardization, but real-world problems are seldom simple enough to be resolved with prefabricated solutions.

76

Is it possible to age gracefully?

Short answer:

Of course!
A building should take
good care of its wrinkles.

Long answer:

Is architecture a mayfly or an elephant? Is it a wonderful insect that flaps its delicate, garish wings for a single summer's day, or a ponderous and wrinkled leviathan with a kind of grace that only a furrowed mountain of skin and muscle can convey? A butterfly dies after a brief life devoted entirely to procreation, while the elephant carries its giant body throughout an unusually long life. We plan our heavy buildings dreaming of the day when they will emerge from their chrysalis and unfurl their brilliant wings before an awestruck world. And sometimes it happens like that. But the building-as-butterfly must survive a metamorphosis every bit as remarkable as the butterfly itself: it has to become, one day, a gorgeous elephant whose beauty only increases with age.

77

Is it more important to follow the style of the place than the style of the time?

Short answer:

Following the place
is the style of our time.

Borlänge, Sweden

Long answer:

A thoughtful interpretation of a place will always appeal to our human need to understand the world around us. Those who succeed in communicating a real sense of a place—any place at all—are sure to have many admirers. Anyone who makes art from the geography of their past is guaranteed to find an audience. It's possible to create buildings that function perfectly well and are at home in any place, such as airports; but generic buildings have a hard time stirring our emotions. No other form of art is so naturally rooted in a place as architecture.

78

Rebellious music often has weight and power. Is there anything similar in architecture?

Short answer:

Revolts are more common on paper than in reality. The real-estate industry is seldom eager for insurrection.

Long answer:

Sure, it's possible to design buildings that kick and scream. As in other arts, there's also an architecture that's driven on by the criticism it sparks. It strives for change, but when that change has been achieved it loses its power. A hundred years ago, Art Nouveau had that kind of oppositional energy, exclaiming, "Out with the impotent architecture of styles and in with the individualistic, expressive, and radical!" But an inflammatory critique is not enough to provide one's work with an objective and a meaning; an architect needs expertise and creativity as well. Architecture that can only be defined in opposition to something else quickly becomes tiresome.

79

Have computers changed architecture?

Short answer:

Surprisingly little.

Long answer:

Computers have had two effects. First, they largely put an end to making drawings and images by hand. Expectations that this would lead to radically more imaginative forms have only been realized in special cases, because most of the work is still in the constructing of the building and those tasks still have to be done largely by hand. Second, the internet has created enormous opportunities to identify several solutions to a given problem. Interpreting an abundance of information is now part of the profession. To sketch is to Google. *That* has changed architecture.

80

Should buildings be visible from a distance?

Short answer:

Not necessarily.
For the most part, it is
the inside that counts.

Long answer:

Whether a building should be visible from far away depends on the circumstances. A building might be most beautiful and striking hiding under a blanket of grass. Another situation might demand a silhouette, a figure outlined against the sky. These two characterizations are exceptions, but no building can avoid the close-up. One reason for the global interest in buildings that are meant to be seen at a distance is that it's cheap: industrialized construction is better at dealing with big gestures. Sensual detailing that's pleasing even to the nearsighted is more demanding of both argumentation and execution.

81

Is there anything more important than energy?

Short answer:

Yes, human dignity.

Halmstad, Sweden

Long answer:

Man impacts the environment wherever we go. If we want to preserve nature untouched, we need to spread out as little as possible and make buildings and communities that limit the effects of our lifestyle. That is a frugal approach, but it won't last if it doesn't allow for a decent life. Energy conservation has become a crucial concern for building. But saving energy is about more than just making buildings air-tight—we know how to do that kind of thing. The real challenge is to produce buildings of such utility that we can get by on less space without losing our dignity. That's a matter of artistic effectiveness.

82

Is Dubai a city?

Short answer:

No, not yet.

Long answer:

The towers of Dubai shoot skyward as if to embody the murky wealth pumped from beneath the earth's crust in the United Arab Emirates. There's no actual need for such towers. After September 11, 2001, however, wealthy Arab investors who no longer felt welcome in the United States prompted a great surge in demand for secure real-estate opportunities closer to home—and for beachfront property. Previous plans for expansion had been directed toward the desert, not into the sea. Massive excavation projects reshaped and multiplied the coastline of the little desert country and an urban steroid shock created the world's most dramatic skyline. If you're looking for public space in streets and plazas, you can only find it in the old parts of the little town built before the hormone injection. It's not clear that Dubai will ever recover from its pumped-up urban planning.

83

All of our new residential buildings look like they've been cloned. Wouldn't a little variation brighten things up?

Short answer:

Yes, variation is an effective way to mask a banal reality.

Long answer:

Trivialities are worse when they come by the dozen. On the other hand, beautiful things become even more beautiful when they come back to us over and over again. Residential architecture has always been built on repetition and many designs end up producing a crushing monotony, instead of creating a charming uniformity. Variation is a cheap way to conceal the fact that you don't have enough money, desire, or knowledge to create real qualities of the kind that stand to be repeated. It is limitation that reveals the true master.

84
What is a room?

Short answer:

Something bounded.
That's beautiful.

Long answer:

It's also a little bit of space. It is, therefore, very limited and yet also unlimited. The unlimited or diffuse space was a modernist ideal that fought against the enclosed room for almost a century. However, the aim was always to create more or less clear boundaries. We need the concept of "space" in order to liberate a room from its floor, its walls, and its ceiling. There aren't many architects today who wouldn't agree that architecture's foremost task is to create spaces, even in the city.

85

How can strict be a compliment?

Short answer:

Sometimes you have to put up with gravity.

Long answer:

Architecture has to be both strict and sensible, just as nature is. The fir's branches divide with rigid consistency in order to utilize the trunk optimally. At the same time, no two trees are identical. That too is a form of optimization —a risk-management strategy that ensures a few individuals will always survive whatever combination of cold, drought, storm, and parasites they encounter each year. A forest of clones is both boring and vulnerable. Nature's diversity is unrelenting. When you design you need to be strict with yourself, not with others. Buildings do well with the kind of consistency that is sometimes called architectural. But then buildings shouldn't all follow the same rules. Strictness and sensitivity—those are good qualities to have.

86

Open or closed floor plan?

Short answer:

Doors and stairs are two of architecture's greatest inventions.

Long answer:

It is true that rooms borrow space from one another in an open floor plan. A small home can feel more spacious if some of the walls are eliminated. But if we go outside, the relationship is the opposite: a small property feels larger if we divide it up into separate spaces. Each one is still pretty big compared to indoor rooms. Often they are also more useful: the delineated area invites us to use it and to care for it. So what happens if we flip the script and turn the house into a garden? It could be like the houses of Pompeii—a dense interior landscape of sunny courtyards and dimly lit rooms in compact clusters.

87

Were modernism's missionaries mistaken?

Short answer:

Yes. The question is whether we know any better today.

Long answer:

Questioning history with the answer in hand isn't fair. The missionaries of modernism had a lot of good reasons for their radical agenda. When the entire world order was changing direction, art, architecture, and urban planning couldn't really continue on as though nothing had happened. But, when a thousand years of development is replaced with simplifications, the results are pretty meager. And the greater the reduction, the less pleasing the result.

Life is not simple and a simple architecture in large scale just doesn't work. There is no form of architecture that can survive elevation to universal law. Buildings can occasionally be pared down to provide simple answers to simple questions. The city never can.

88

What is parametric design?

Short answer:

When form follows data.

Borlänge, Sweden

Long answer:

The hull of a sailboat is formed by the interaction among certain variables, including its length, breadth and depth, the shape of the bow, stern and keel, and the laws of hydrodynamics. The curve of each rib is generated as a function of these parameters. Computers are outstanding at calculating such complex forms, but boat builders and stone carvers alike have worked with parametric design for centuries. Cutting a piece of stone in a quarry to fit perfectly into some faraway cupola requires both a method of making complex calculations and a method of describing them. Like today's computer-generated models, these can be impressive, but the art of designing space has little to do with calculations. If the architect doesn't choose the correct parameters, the result will seem ad hoc. The most fundamental parameters of architecture are man and his senses.

89

Is the architect an authoritarian?

Short answer:

No. Don't confuse the responsibility of proposing solutions with the power to execute them.

Long answer:

Few things have changed the role of the architect as radically as when many people lost faith in the idea of authority in the 1970s. Nothing was the same after that. Numerous star architects born around the turn of the last century, such as Alvar Aalto, had become fixtures in the architectural firmament, but fell hard to earth when the society that had held them aloft suddenly turned its back on all establishment figures. The revolt against the status quo changed the rules of the game for architects and politicians in particular. And the loss of authority soon led to the loss of self-confidence, but that's nothing to grumble about now. The days when an architect could lead the way by pointing are long gone; now it's essential to be enthusiastic and encourage everyone to come together. That works best if architects believe in themselves.

90

Why all these changes? Can't architects just do it right from the start?

Short answer:

No. Designing is learning.

Long answer:

You must always dare to change your mind, because nobody knows everything from the start. A sketch is nothing but a collection of knowledge. The complexity of the design arises—or should arise—as lessons are learned. Almost every building project is framed by conflicts. Some of these can be devastating enough to make the project's original strengths melt away, but most conflicts force an examination of the weak spots and make the project better. I am not sure, but I think uncertainty may be the essence of the creative process.

91

Why build a model when we have computers?

Short answer:

Because it's a small
step closer to reality.

Boxholm, Sweden

Long answer:

Architecture moves in multiple dimensions, and pictures can only describe fragments. A model can teach the observer something. A little model made of cardboard or wood can be examined by many people who are together in the same space, while a computer-generated virtual model is better suited to individual exploration. However, all models—scientific conceptual models as well as physical construction models—share the ability to communicate knowledge about a corner of reality. The experiences we glean from that knowledge can be used to make improvements, which means that, whether its virtual or actual, one model is never enough. You need to look at a lot of different models before you've seen all there is to see.

92
Is five better than four?

Short answer:

Yes, for the most part.

Long answer:

The importance of numerical mysticism in
the great religions is nothing to be surprised
about. Numbers also play a central role in the
man-made environment. Even numbers can
be hard to deal with. Regularity can be banal;
sometimes the space between elements is more
important than the elements themselves. An
even number of objects always gives you an odd
number of spaces. The number one is a universe
unto itself. With the number two, a dynamic
begins, but there is no complexity until three.
The number four creates an enclosed group
in every case. And five suggests the possibility
of a continuation, seven even more so. At eight
we reach the border between a gathering of
individuals and a crowd. We cannot grasp
larger numbers than this without counting the
elements one by one.

93

Some buildings are hard to understand. What should I do?

Short answer:

Believe your eyes.
The building is probably strange.

Vaggeryd, Sweden

Long answer:

Music and architecture are languages that cross time and space. A sanctuary built a thousand years ago is full of religious messages that few people can understand today without interpretation. But, beyond the obsolete decorations, there is an architecture that anyone can relate to, and measurements that largely are the same anywhere and anytime. A room of about 12 by 12 feet, or 3.5 by 3.5 meters, can be used for any domestic purpose, and is therefore to be found all over the world in abundant variations. Real masterpieces, no matter how ordinary they may be, are enjoyed by all. Few architects are gifted with the talent to design their buildings with the ease of the vernacular.

94
What is an architect?

Short answer:

A chief builder.

Long answer:

Perhaps surprisingly, the word *architect* has nothing to do with the word *arch*. The ancient Greek root of the first part of the word has the same meaning as in archbishop, that is, "the chief." The second part refers to a builder or carpenter, and is also the root of the word *technology*. The Greeks also used it as a verb: "Architect us, guide us," wrote Aristophanes. *Tectonic* is still a way to describe a building's organization (a quality that set-design, for example, does not have). In the past, the word "architectonic" was used to describe a building's artistic structure. Now that the title "architect" is being used by people who plan computer systems or negotiate agreements, it is perhaps time to start talking again about the chief builder, the leader.

95

Doesn't the answer lie in the surroundings?

Short answer:

The site must, in any event, be better as a result of the architect's work than it was before.

Long answer:

The interpretation that new buildings ought to be adapted to their surroundings is a relatively new idea that emerged in architectural discourse for the first time in Milan in the 1950s. This notion eventually had a tremendous influence over both national and international policy documents. But it's not a watertight model. There is a risk that the new addition to a site is just a lesser version of the surrounding context. If an environment is too dismal, the architect needs to break free of it. The question should always be about which framing elements to follow. The masters of the Baroque era in Rome saw nothing wrong with recreating everything all at once. With imagination and fantasy they coaxed an entirely new architecture into the antique fabric of the city. It's harder than you might think to listen and talk at the same time.

96

Is there a difference between a road and a street?

Short answer:

Roads are faster; streets are slower.

Long answer:

None of the decisions we make about our cities is more important than those that determine how we move through them. In the 1930s, the short, low pedestrian bridges that linked together many cities' waterfront edges began to be replaced with longer and higher bridges for cars. That brought roads into the heart of the city. While a street is full of destinations, a road simply connects two destinations. With the new bridges and their on- and off-ramps, those two destinations could end up quite far apart, farther than was convenient for walking. This, in turn, shaped the built environment. Nothing has had a greater impact on the modern city than the car.

97

Who decides what architecture is?

Short answer:

The trusted, the elected,
and those with the money.

Long answer:

It would be nice to answer that we all do, but it's really not that simple. In many contexts, there is someone who finally decides. Municipalities have antiquarians and architects who draw up the outlines for what deserves to be preserved and what can be permitted for construction. Despite their learned expertise, these two groups often come into conflict with each other. The antiquarians defend the tracks of history, while the architects want to make new tracks. Hopefully, both are acting in the public interest, but the architect's reasoning is always more abstract. The challenge of coming to an agreement about what *is* architecture cannot compare to the question of what can *become* architecture. That is the core of the architect's expertise.

98

Wouldn't it be natural for buildings to be a little softer?

Short answer:

The flat horizon belongs to nature too.

Vissefjärda, Sweden

Long answer:

The vision of making buildings that suit
their purpose like a snail in its shell is as
old as architecture itself, but the logic of
orthogonality is just as reasonable. And therein
lies architecture's eternally vital conflict. The
master builders of the Gothic era had rational
ideas that went beyond the straight line and
right angle. The technological twentieth century
was framed by curving and sweeping forms,
first in the waves of Art Nouveau and later in
computer-generated coral-like structures. But
the search for an organic architecture does not
have to lead to billowing sea-kelp forms; the
world is complex enough as it is. The challenge
is to design a form that fits, not to force round
pegs into square holes.

99

What would a checklist of all the desirable qualities be like?

Short answer:

Contradictory.

Long answer:

Architecture is made up of choices. Beautiful buildings block the view. Elegant, thin façades waste a lot of energy. Pleasantly enclosed spaces prevent people from taking the shortest way through. Monumental buildings diminish their surroundings. It's not easy to choose. A checklist can never weigh the options for you; only experience can do that. And yet there is no end to the lists, quality controls, and certifications. But it's not good enough merely to check off every box on the environmental list. All architecture today must be quality controlled, but that doesn't mean that all quality-controlled architecture is good.

100

Any advice about how to make home a little nicer?

Short answer:

Try contrasts and uniformity.

Long answer:

Let the children have the room closest to the entrance—they're the ones with the most active social life. Walk-through rooms should be avoided, but the opportunity to walk a circuit around the home always feels liberating. A decent amount of counter space—at least three feet, or a meter—between the sink and the stove-top is also nice. If there's an opportunity to plan the home with interesting sight-lines through the spaces, that's always a good quality, and so is letting the daylight in from as many directions as possible. Rooms that face the cold morning light can have cool colors and those with evening light can have warmer tones. Changes in elevation give the home an extra dimension; nothing creates as much dignity as a high ceiling and nothing makes a room feel more intimate than a low one. And a little niche onto a large room seldom feels wrong.

101

What does architecture do for us?

Short answer:

It gives you comfort, joy, affirmation, and company.

Long answer:

You can't fill every place with people. In any city, half-empty streets will always be the norm. In the country, the emptiness can be even more tangible. Architecture is there by your side when you need it most, with the presence of those who have been there before and the promise that others will come by before long, even if you're alone at the moment. It's not just about expanding "urban" patterns. It goes beyond the mantra of creating "meeting places." Architecture is about sharing the comfort of human society.

Index of Questions

1. Why is the world most beautiful at twilight?

2. Thresholds: wouldn't it be nice to get rid of them?

3. How long will modernity be dressed in glass?

4. When does architecture become sensual?

5. Can't we design buildings to look like they used to?

6. Do buildings really have memories?

7. What makes cities so fascinating?

8. Doesn't technology determine everything?

9. What caused the crisis in architecture?

10. Is there some kind of universal formula?

11. Do architects have to think of everything?

12. How long should buildings last?

13. Buildings frame our lives. But can life ever be predictable?

14. Someone took my idea. Should I be upset?

15. Are natural materials better than imitations?

16. Does history have a future?

17. Can architecture be mass-produced?

18. Is architecture necessary?

19. Does architecture develop?

20. How can an architect become famous?

21. Why do people look at buildings when they're traveling?

22. I read all the magazines and blogs. Is there anything I might have overlooked?

23. Does it have to be expensive?

24. Can you own a view?

25. Is it important to get published?

26. Do books give you a sharper view?

27. What protects us from becoming blind to everyday wonders?

28. What do buildings sound like?

29. Are all churches architecture?

30. Why do architects want to paint the world white?

31. Can a rich architecture be affordable?

32. What is the worst thing about architecture today?

33. What is the best thing about architecture today?

34. How is a beautiful façade composed?

35. What is the point of regulations?

36. Is architecture the spice of life or its sustenance?

37. Is higher density always a good thing?

38. Art always wants to do the opposite. Is it the same with architecture?

39. Should architects build on the best place on the site?

40. Who was the first architect?

41. How are the conditions for architecture where I live?

42. Is it strange that we long to get away sometimes?

43. Must we demolish beautiful buildings and scenic vistas in order to urbanize?

44. A swimming pool lined with fake fur? Sounds terrible, doesn't it?

45. What is the cleverest way to save money?

46. Why is there so much prestige attached to an opera house?

47. What is stone?

48. Why are ruins so beautiful?

49. What is architecture?

50. What does urban mean?

51. Why is it so hard to make good cities?

52. What is the point of architectural competitions?

53. Is it okay to repeat yourself?

54. The opportunities seem infinite. If an architect could highlight just one quality, what should it be?

55. Where does form come from?

56. What role does politics play?

57. Has architecture become international?

58. Does a place have a soul?

59. What is the world's most admired building?

60. How small can a home be?

61. How do architects win competitions?

62. What is a good plan?

63. Is there something special about marble?

64. Why is uncompromising architecture so good?

65. Why is uncompromising architecture so bad?

66. What is the point of details?

67. What is the significance of tuberculosis?

68. I like interiors that are bright and cheery. Who doesn't?

69. What is noise?

70. What makes old factories so cool?

71. Is architecture natural?

72. Do buildings have character?

73. Are words necessary? Isn't it enough just to design?

74. Does architecture have a moral?

75. What is simplicity?

76. Is it possible to age gracefully?

77. Is it more important to follow the style of the place than the style of the time?

78. Rebellious music often has weight and power. Is there anything similar in architecture?

79. Have computers changed architecture?

80. Should buildings be visible from a distance?

81. Is there anything more important than energy?

82. Is Dubai a city?

83. All of our new residential buildings look like they've been cloned. Wouldn't a little variation brighten things up?

84. What is a room?

85. How can strict be a compliment?

86. Open or closed floor plan?

87. Were modernism's missionaries mistaken?

88. What is parametric design?

89. Is the architect an authoritarian?

90. Why all these changes? Can't architects just do it right from the start?

91. Why build a model when we have computers?

92. Is five better than four?

93. Some buildings are hard to understand. What should I do?

94. What is an architect?

95. Doesn't the answer lie in the surroundings?

96. Is there a difference between a road and a street?

97. Who decides what architecture is?

98. Wouldn't it be natural for buildings to be a little softer?

99. What would a checklist of all the desirable qualities be like?

100. Any advice about how to make home a little nicer?

101. What does architecture do for us?

Notes

Most of the thoughts in this book are our own reflections on our built environment. Most of these come from common knowledge and some of them are taken from Rasmus Wærn's previous writings. Those that emerge more directly from other sources are listed below.

1. The idea that we need help to grow as humans from childhood through adolescence and into adults is taken from the German thinker Friedrich von Hügel (1852–1925) and in particular his book *The Mystical Element in Religion* (1908).

16. The three uses of history is a lesson we learned from Professor Johan Mårtelius at the KTH Royal Institute of Technology, Stockholm.

18. The image of the greedy people in the beautiful town was something Alvar Aalto picked up from Anatole France's novel, *At the Sign of the Reine Pédauque* (*La Rôtisserie de la reine Pédauque*, 1893). Aalto referenced the idea in a lecture given March 6, 1925, at a gala evening of the Jyväskylä Student Union, as quoted by Göran Schildt in *Alvar Aalto in His Own Words* (1997).

21. The difference between art and architecture is one of Adolf Loos's one-liners. It was first published in his essay "Architecture" ("Architektur," 1910).

22. The French philosopher Gaston Bachelard (1884–1962) was the main proponent of this idea of the "poetics of space" (which also was the title of one of his books).

23. Architect Léonie Geisendorf talked over the relation between parsimony and austerity in a famous lecture in 1963, which was printed under the title "Om sparsamheten" in the Swedish review of architecture, *Arkitektur*, in December of the same year.

26. August Strindberg's short story was named "Rome in a Day" and was first published in his collection *Things Published and Unpublished* (*Tryckt och otryckt*, 1890–91).

30. Among the architects and artists that have adopted the principle of coloring relating to the sun are Bruno Taut (1880–1938) and Poul Gernes (1925–96).

40. Imhotep, commonly referred as "the first architect," was in fact the son of the royal architect Kanofer, according to Lyon Sprague de Camp, author of *The Ancient Engineers* (1963).

46. It was the German author and critic Johann Christoph Gottsched who, in the 1760s, wrote that "*In Berlin heißt das Ding jetzt* Publikum" (In Berlin the thing [the audience] is now called the public) in a daily paper, quoted in Eduard Engel's 1908 history of German literature. Jürgen Habermas references this in *The Structural Transformation of the Public Sphere* (*Strukturwandel der Öffentlichkeit. Untersuchungen zu einer Kategorie der bürgerlichen Gesellschaft*, 1962).

49. *Den byggda bilden av oss själva* (*The Built Image of Ourself*, 1991) was the title of a collection of essays by Stefan Alenius.

67. According to the Center for Disease Control in the United States, it is estimated that two billion people worldwide (one third of the global population) are currently infected with the bacteria that causes tuberculosis.

72. The creator of this catalogue of characters was Jacques-François Blondel (1705–74) who included it in his multi-volume printed curriculum for the Académie d'Architecture *(Cours d'Architecture*, 1771–77). Adrian Forty pointed this out in his own comprehensive book, *Words and Buildings* (2000).

75. The magazine most associated with marketing the unusual usual was the Italian *Domus*, during Vittorio Magnago Lampugnani's time at the helm.

76. "The Elephant and the Butterfly" is a fairy tale by E.E. Cummings as well as the title of the 9th Alvar Aalto seminar (international symposiums on architecture, held every three years at the Alvar Aalto museum) in 2003.

77. The words that it is more important to follow the place than the time are Gunnar Asplund's (1885–1940), published in *Arkitektur* (October 1916).

95. The idea that buildings ought to be adapted to their surroundings was promoted by the magazine *Casabella*, under the editorial direction of Ernesto Nathan Rogers.

Rasmus Wærn and Gert Wingårdh are two
Swedish architects who are working to try to
make architecture better—Rasmus with words
and Gert with actions. One of them has tried
to understand and explain why buildings
look the way they do, often using architectural
history as a tool, while the other has designed
buildings all over Sweden and in many other
places. They have made books together
before, including *Crucial Words: Conditions
for Contemporary Architecture*.

You can contact them at
rasmus.waern@wingardhs.se
and gert.wingardh@wingardhs.se

Rasmus Wærn (left) and Gert Wingårdh (right)